Learning to Read, Step by Step!

Ready to Read   Preschool–Kindergarten
• big type and easy words • rhyme and rhythm • picture clues
For children who know the alphabet and are eager to
begin reading.

Reading with Help   Preschool–Grade 1
• basic vocabulary • short sentences • simple stories
For children who recognize familiar words and sound out
new words with help.

Reading on Your Own   Grades 1–3
• engaging characters • easy-to-follow plots • popular topics
For children who are ready to read on their own.

Reading Paragraphs   Grades 2–3
• challenging vocabulary • short paragraphs • exciting stories
For newly independent readers who read simple sentences
with confidence.

Ready for Chapters   Grades 2–4
• chapters • longer paragraphs • full-color art
For children who want to take the plunge into chapter books
but still like colorful pictures.

STEP INTO READING® is designed to give every child a successful
reading experience. The grade levels are only guides; children will progress
through the steps at their own speed, developing confidence in their reading.

Remember, a lifetime love of reading starts with a single step!

To Dr. Henry Wilbur,
a fun herpetologist

*The editors would like to thank Jim Breheny, Director Bronx Zoo and EVP of
WCS Zoos & Aquarium, New York, for his assistance in the preparation of this book.*

*The authors would like to thank Nicole Tunstall, MSc, and Ashley Margaret Miller for their help
in creating this book.*

Visit us on the Web!
StepIntoReading.com
randomhousekids.com

Educators and librarians, for a variety of teaching tools, visit us at
RHTeachersLibrarians.com

ISBN 978-0-553-50775-1 (trade) — ISBN 978-0-553-50776-8 (lib. bdg.) —
ISBN 978-0-553-50777-5 (ebook)

Printed in the United States of America
10 9 8 7 6 5 4 3 2 1

Random House Children's Books supports the First Amendment and celebrates the right to read.

Wild Reptiles
Snakes,
Crocodiles, Lizards,
and Turtles!

WILD KRATTS

by Martin Kratt and Chris Kratt

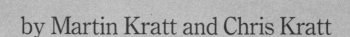

Random House 🏠 New York

Imagine if you could do what reptiles do.

You could crawl, climb,
or slither just like them.

But what are reptiles?

Most reptiles hatch from eggs.

Reptiles have scales.

Reptiles are cold-blooded.

That means they need the sun
to get warm.

Crocodiles and alligators,
lizards, snakes, and turtles
are all reptiles.

Let's learn more about them.

Activate Creature Powers!

Rattlesnakes!

A rattlesnake has special scales on its tail.

The scales are used
to make a rattling sound.
The sound is a warning
that the snake wants
to be left alone.

Rattlesnakes have long fangs.
They use their fangs
to catch food and
defend themselves.
Venom comes through
the fangs when they strike.

The venom is poisonous.

"Watch out!"

Martin warns a coyote.

Crocodiles!

The Nile crocodile is one of
the biggest reptiles!
It is not afraid of
the hippos and lions
that also use the river.

A Nile crocodile has
more than 60 teeth.
"Open wide!" says Chris.

A mother crocodile is gentle
with her babies.
She watches over them
and protects them.

She even carries them
carefully in her jaws.
"This is a fun way to travel,"
says Martin.

Draco Lizards!

A Draco lizard has wing-like structures that unfold from its sides to help it move through the air.

It can glide from tree to tree.

Jump! Glide! Land!

"Dracos make it look easy.

I need more practice,"

says Chris.

Basilisk Lizards!

Many reptiles swim.
Only one can run
on top of the water!

The basilisk lizard
has big webbed feet.
Its feet move so fast,
it can run across the water
without sinking.

"Wait for me!" shouts Chris.

Gila Monsters!

These lizards mostly
live underground.
They only come up
for sun, water, and food.

"Nice to get out once in a while," says Martin.

Rock Pythons!

A python is a constricting
snake.
It wraps around its prey
and squeezes,
then swallows it whole!

Rock pythons live in holes on the African savannah. They eat gazelles and warthogs.

"Want me to untangle you now?" asks Martin.

Geckos!

Geckos are small lizards
with a big Creature Power.

A gecko has special toes that can hold on to almost any surface. Even glass!

Turtles!

There are more than 300 different kinds of turtles and tortoises— with one creature power in common: a shell!

It helps to protect them
when they are in danger.
The Tortuga is shaped
like a turtle.
It protects the
Wild Kratts.

Alligators!

Alligators are related
to crocodiles,
but they have wide snouts.
Crocodiles have pointy,
narrow snouts.

Alligator

Crocodile

Alligators are
grayish black.
Crocodiles are
brownish green.
Both creatures can grow
to be very big.

"Later, gator!" says Chris.

"In a while, crocodile!"

Martin replies.

Go, Creature Powers!